D-June 14th, 2016~ Day 1

I never intended for this to be real
To actually give up
To throw in some metaphorical towel that I never needed
Because what's to dry off if I never actually jumped in?

I gave up on my first day
Gave up on love
Gave up on forgiveness
Even gave up on progress
Because nothing seems to have real purpose anymore

There's no point
No plot
No story
Really nothing.
Things change but only how could they not?

Time is a shark that always moves forward but never back
Always gets more deadly as it runs out and gets nearer
And my time is far from up
Though there are times I wish it wasn't
But that's all part of the package.
Wishing for clocks to unwind or wind in a different direction
Hoping for the winds of change to morph into a tornado of good karma
Though nothing can be done when my well of hope runs out
It's almost dry this time.
199 days.

Love.
The one thing I'd craved most in the world
Was the one thing I gave up on because it didn't love me back

It came in different forms to me
As a family I'd been born into
That drifted before it was ever together

As a young visionary
With a beautiful mind and unforgiving willpower
But hasn't done anything but gave me a taste of it's wonders
And now I'm hooked

I'm completely in control
I only lose myself to it every once in a while
When everything around me is hopeless
And the possibility of someone or something loving me back isn't as
crazy as it seems
When I can't wake myself
Because the imaginary arms surrounding me feel so warm
And the lines I read between never abandon me
I lose myself a little...

But then disaster strikes
In those words
Those evil words made specially to feed my desire
Constructed to hit a chord buried inside of me
Swirl around my head whenever I read them
And he says things to me he's said ten times before
And he writes the things I have thought about a million nights or more
And he answers questions that fill my head
Then uses his beautiful words to make me wait
Hours and days go by and I'm found again

But he utters a word and I'm without direction
Spins a phrase and I'm a puddle for him to wipe his mouth with
And I know I am heartless
My chest empty except for these fragile strings
And he'll speak this word disguised love
And strike every note I wish didn't exist
And I want to want him to stop
But I can't.

He's played my strings.
He's played me and won.
And I've never heard sweeter or sadder music.

B-June 16th, 2016~Day 3

There's an absence of words
Because there's so much confusion
Because people do so much for so little
Because when anything is said for small gain
I can't bring myself to speak.

There isn't a line to draw
When there's already a border in place
I can't understand love from miles away
Or through a screen
When the only connection is when we are connected
Through Wi-Fi or data
Through an app where a double tapped red heart
Can somehow mean just as much as pouring a real one out
I simply can't understand

G-June 17th, 2016~Day 4

There's always that saying
"Don't sweat the small stuff"
But that's what should matter
The little things that happen each day

The things we blink and miss
The small wonders that we don't have until they're lost
There's something about them that make each day brighter

Putting your glasses on and seeing so clearly
Pushing the hair from your face so you don't miss a sunrise
Humming an invisible song to pass the time

The things that go unnoticed
Are the ones that build us up
They make us strong
They make the day strong
And any strong day is one more worth living

R-June 18th, 2016~ Day 5

The first five days were more bad than good, but by day 5 I don't feel as bad as I thought. Getting it down takes the weight off of my shoulders, even if it doesn't completely turn around how I'm feeling. It's weird how the things that have happened since I've started this project have affected me so much it's made it easier to have words to put down, even when I didn't know how to. Today was filled with a lot more disappointment than I would've liked, but it wasn't completely lost. I'm not giving up hope, and I'm hoping the next 195 days are better :)

B-June 19th, 2016~ Day 6

Waking up with disappointment
A soul crushing realization
That trust does not exist
And promises really are made to be broken

Something seeming so small
Holds a crushing weight on my shoulders
And curses me before I can curse myself.
I should have known better
A wolf in sheep's clothing always bets the devil it's head
Though even the devil stood as a false prophet, right?

Thinking it would pan out somehow was naive
Hoping things would change is just plain evil
And fooling myself was inevitable
Though I'll never live and learn

G-June 20th, 2016~Day 7

Another day of disappointment
But forcing myself into productivity
Like so many others before me
Isn't as much of a fairytale as I thought.

It changed the void
Instead of filled with emptiness and sorrow
It overflowed with anger
A good anger that made me want to make something other than
excuses

The anger churning and taming every now and then
Like a sleeping dragon housed in my chest waiting to unleash a scorching
flame
Maybe I've gone too far
Turned into a monster

But so far I can't find a problem with that
Better to turn into a different monster than the one you'll never defeat

D-June 21st, 2016~Day 8

A sleepless night
A river of tears
A mind full of panic

Don't think I've ever felt that alone
And at such an ungodly hour
No one was around to disagree
So all of the silence fed my madness

I still can't shake the weight my body carries
Like lead in summer clothes
And have tried drowning my heaviness
But submerging my head on floated the sadness
And I couldn't stay under forever.

I ended it by rocking myself to sleep
Telling myself that I'm not alone
Chanting that I am okay
Because I don't know if I'll ever not need someone else
But I'm too fragile to be on my own
And to afraid not to be

G-June 22nd, 2016~Day 9

I tasted the sun today
I felt summer
And felt the warmth melt all of my nerves when I stepped through the door
Saw the smiles
Heard the excitement of my arrival

I was ready
The first real happiness I've had in a while
The first breath of fun I've gotten to soak up since I can remember
And I'd do it all again without changing a thing.

I swam like I was weightless
Ate and laughed like I meant it
Almost like in a movie
Where happy endings exist
And people love each other
Where you wish to see someone again and it comes true.

It stayed daylight until nighttime
And I finally watched a fire burn through a sunset
The sky paint pretty colors
And felt calmer and surer than I've ever felt.
I felt summer

R-June 24th, 2016~ Day 10 reflection

In the last 10 days, I've seen myself reach one of the darkest nights I've had in a long time. But at the same time, I've felt genuine happiness. So it's extremely frustrating so far, but I still don't feel a weight on my shoulders anymore, and trying to be honest and poetic is a... stylistic challenge at best, though I can't say it isn't working. And, it's kind of weird, but the metaphors I've used have a bit of accuracy to them. I still don't feel motivated to do much, and I'm still butterfly wings, but getting it out is still proven effective.

G-Friday, June 24th, 2016~Day 11

Today another adventure brews
It's one I've taken before
And it began with a rockier start than usual.

Tomorrow I make a choice
I find out if I can be a hero
If I can save someone with just myself
And when I first thought to save them
It barely crossed my mind
And that felt good

I like feeling good
Especially for someone else.
Maybe this won't all be in vain after all

G- Saturday, June 25th, 2016~Day 12

Today felt long
But I got to see a familiar face
Fell in a desire to be closer to a forbidden one
And felt the disappointment of missing yet another

But everything was relatively quiet.
Not as lethal as radio silence
But not loud and nuclear and terrifying
It was calm.
Content.
I felt good for a while

I let myself over think
And felt the dark snake of a feeling hovering over me
Threatening to eliminate the warmth I'd let roam inside of me
But I was reminded of my strength
I remembered to let go
To breathe
And it didn't get the chance to suffocate me

Though it came pretty close.

G-June 26th, 2016~ Day 13

Today we celebrate an anniversary
I question my dedication to this very day
But celebrate nonetheless

I return home to comfort
Go back to where I am not afraid
And feel bliss in a long car ride
I can't bring myself to sleep
But I'm too tired for creativity right now-A serious tragedy

I can't wait to wrap myself in blankets
And plant myself in front of a screen to fill with words
And sit in the dark and waste time
All of these meaningless things I can do are so worth doing
When there's no fear of judgement
When I can be happier and actually mean it

B- Monday, June 27th, 2016-Day 14

I woke up to someone today
 With an interest in me
Or rather in my body
I didn't think anything of it, it always turns out the same
But this one was different
This one started off decent

Made me think better intentions were had
Even kept their cool for a short while
After only a few hours
A few exchanges
A few crucial reveals
And then he said he loved me
But I'd given up on that already so I felt nothing

But he claimed to feel everything
Was already making promises
Already claiming me as his "forever"
And I was already getting cold feet
More frigid than the chills this gave

I could tell this would-be poison
That I'd made a mistake
And this joke of a commitment had left me frozen with fear
Because what about the things I had done?
What I said back?
It wasn't as bad but it didn't leave me innocent
Didn't allow me to play the victim

It's too toxic
And It hasn't been a full day yet
It's a toxin from thousands of miles away
But I can still feel it sinking in
Paralyzing me
And I'm in too deep to quit

R-Tuesday, June 28th, 2016~ Day 15

      Externalizing everything that's happened somehow sparked an influx of events good and bad that sometimes have me questioning e v e r y t h i n g, and it makes it harder to write these because then I wonder if it's even real at this point. I stopped keeping track of the times because it seems irrelevant. I don't think time is a factor in this anymore, not with all the stuff that's been going down lately. Knowing that someone or someone's will read these makes me anxious and almost afraid but at the same time it's really liberating. Like, someone hearing what it's like living like this and how different things impact it will make it real, make it better somehow. So, as of Day 15, I have no honest idea of how this is going, but I've got 185 days to go.

G- Wednesday, June 29th, 2016~ Day 16

It's like Christmas eve
The one I should've had
Spent at home instead of in an ER
White snow instead of white floors

And I could care less about presents or Santa
Because I get a new chance to welcome someone back into my life
The one person that I've forgiven over and over
The only person I could've cut from my life forever with no trouble

But I never did
And I'm glad

It's like my wedding day
I'm promising myself to a new life
The one coming back is the one giving me away
And my something old & something new
The only thing borrowed is time
Time, we can finally get back.

It's like a reset button's been hit
And we're getting another chance

It's like my father's come back
And this time he's here to stay

G- Thursday, June 17th, 2016~ Day 17

Nothing is harder than trying to refit into a different mold
After years of formation
And then an adjustment period
Coming back to the original fit
Is something so needed and necessary
Words haven't been created to describe it!

And just when you'd think it couldn't get better it does!
And with the simplest things
Watching a practice in warm silence
Washing a car
And waiting for food
Even buying ice brightened every part of today as much as anything else

Every little thing felt bigger and better
Because not a second was wasted
And not a minute went unappreciated

G- Friday, July 1st, 2016~Day 18

Sometimes I feel like happy days are fantasies
And then here they are
So real and even tangible I can't begin to take them in enough

At the beach when time stops
And the sand is always cool
And the water always feels comforting

I wish everyday was like the beach
Like today.

B-Saturday, July 2nd, 2016~Day 19

Sometimes I get really happy
And I take pictures
Keepsakes.
And I make wallpapers
Memories.

And it all comes flooding back
All the things that make me happy
So I can keep myself afloat

But it only lasts for a little
Then I get so... Sad
Like those things don't matter
Like they can't save me
Like they can't last

And I'm trying to stay with the happy
I'm trying to float
But I just can't shake the feeling that
Nothing DOES last forever
And happiness doesn't even make it half that long.

Because I wake up at sunset
And I sleep when the only light comes from the moon
And I can't help but feel like I'm watching the days pass me by
After I've barely made it through the nights

R- Sunday July 3rd, 2016~ Day 20

I'm really glad he's back, and it's nice knowing where he is and being a bit spoiled, but I'm still afraid things are going to go back to how they were and I don't think I can take that. And I've realized that I'm happiest with myself when I'm making others happy in toxic ways. Not so toxic that I'll stop, but somehow poisonous enough that I know what I'm doing. I wonder how long it'll be until I fall apart again.

G- Monday, July 4th, 2016~ Day 21

Today's a day I've always celebrated
But it's been such a terrible year
So much telling me it's not freedom at all

But maybe today's different?
Today we're almost whole
Almost a family
And I can live with that

-Tuesday, July 5th, 2016~Day 22

Days like this pass me by
In a lull of fading sun and laughs
And I stay cooped up inside
Away from nothing in particular

Maybe from talking
Probably hiding.
Hiding from talking things to death
Frankly anything that isn't comfortable silence scares me lately
Though I'm somehow growing louder and bolder
But at the same time can't face my own fears
And words disappear when they stare me in the face

B-Wednesday, July 6th, 2016~Day 23

I'm filled with rage
My eyes fill with tears at every black man filled with bullets
My spirit is thrown
At every black woman thrown to the ground

Squashed under the boots of a white man
White men
I've feared
I've shaken my head
But I've never seen so closely
So CLEARLY
A life snatched
Torn
Eliminated
So quickly
So remorselessly

This won't be the end
How am I supposed to go on?
You'd think we'd move past this
You'd be wrong

D- Thursday, July 7th, 2016~Day 24

Today I got up
At 12:00am
I hugged my sister and told her happy birthday
Because she got to see it this year
But what I saw after made me feel almost rotten.

Another black man shot.
"Another black man"
That's what they'll call him
Won't say his name
But the number of convictions
Won't show his high school yearbook
But will look for his mugshot

Won't arrest the officer
But his girlfriend
Who watched him bleed
Who showed the world
Who told their daughter to close her eyes from the backseat?
Who repeated the events out loud to make them real?

Was thrown on the ground in handcuffs

I saw him lay across the seat
His arm mangled with the bullets black America must bite
That officer screaming
That officer probably afraid
That officer with no regret
That officer who'd taken a life and scarred a child

Broke a family
Angered us all

And then I turned my sister away from the television
Happy Birthday

R- Friday, July 8th, 2016~Day 25

I feel so completely numb. And afraid, and just can't stop thinking about how shitty everything is about to get. There are officers dead now and everyone is blaming black people and the BLM movement and I just can't understand how because they tell us not to blame all cops when cops all over are killing us with no punishment and who knows what's going to happen? A race war? A civil war? A mass exodus???? Who can tell?! I feel so hopeless in these days with no money or presence to give and all I can do is repost something or rant and I don't know if that'll be enough? If I'll get through this alive or content and if my family in other places will be okay. I can't help but be afraid. Why isn't it safe to be black anymore? I've been so depressed about it I haven't been moving. I haven't been doing anything. But hoping.

D- Saturday, July 9th, 2016~Day 26

I haven't really shut my eyes
At least not for that long
It's hard to sleep while so conscious
While everything's going wrong

Everything falling apart
Like the end is coming
And what can stop it?
Nothing and no one.
It's pretty much hopeless
And it's not at all over

D- Sunday, July 10th, 2016~Day 27

I covered myself in black today
Because many have fallen
And though they are far I still feel as though I'm living in a funeral

And I listened to someone that shared my skin but not my beliefs
And I listened to others teach their children to not be afraid
And I listened to them tell us that even though many are dying for select reasons
Everyone still matters
But I didn't speak
I couldn't
The lies left me speechless and they weren't even mine

They belonged to those above me
They were fed to those below me
And I refuse to be a part of either

G-Monday, July 11th, 2016~Day 28

I forgot.
Everything that's happened
That could happen
I forgot.

I got the chance to laugh again
With the people I've needed for so long
And I started something I could love

I bit my tongue more than once
But that's nothing compared to the release I've felt today
Even for just a little while.

B-Tuesday, July 12th~Day 29

Every time I wake up warm
I panic
I fall asleep so cold and certain
It astonishes me how I awaken so confused

Like where I'm laying doesn't belong with me
What I'm dreaming doesn't feel right
But I'm not going to change anything
The sadness is the beginning
Especially since it's all coming to an end anyhow

But everything is blurring together
In one giant senseless memory
Pointless

R-Wednesday, July 13th, 2016~Day 30

These past two weeks have been extremely hard and nothing's even happening to me. I can't tell if I've proved my thesis because it's all being forced out of me at the wrong times. Every time I try and sit myself down to write something, I can't. It helps to just furiously type out my emotions, but being so late says something somehow. All of the death and fear has infected me, like part of me has died, or something less dramatic has happened. It's like admitting to something I don't want to face yet. I guess more than anything I'm tired, like that's the only word I can use to describe what I feel. I found a good distraction this week, something to liven me up. I hope it lasts and I won't end up screwing up this whole thing before it gets going.

G-Thursday, July 14th, 2016~Day 31

I've learned something this week
You pick a pattern
Make sure it fits you and only you
Then you pin it down so it can't escape you
Cut it out so you won't forget
Pin it again and stitch together

Surge it up nice and tight so it'll last forever
Then pin it down for a final time so you know you mean it
Tear it up just a bit and string it up
Stretch it
Let it breathe
The slip it on and feel what you've accomplished
By yourself
For yourself

You've just made a big decision.

G-Friday, July 15th, 2016~Day 32

I wash my hands of sadness for a while
I can finally relax
I've become numb to sounds of gunfire
But can also accept that things may not change

I got to forget for just a little while
And everyone should have that
Someone to let you forget
Someone to give you something you never thought you wanted

I'd never admit it before
But ignorance truly is bliss.

G-Saturday, July 16th, 2016~Day 33

I've longed for adventure
But find too much comfort here
Not enough to keep me chained down
But I feel content

I have enough patience to count the tiles
To listen to wind chimes carry out senseless songs
Like a new high's been reached for such a short time
Because these things don't ever last
They just remain as memories
I guess the best ones often do?

G-Sunday, July 17th, 2016~Day 34

I can somehow find peace in the strong detestation I hold
Such big words for a simple feeling
But it makes the most sense
I get to share something wonderful with everyone

Even if I must listen to crippling arrogance not deserved

So dramatic am I
To act as if I am being tortured
Held against my will.
It's true I have little choice
But I'd never let that stop me

I can't question no faith of mine
It cannot be shaken
Only stirred

I could almost do this again.

R-Monday, July 18th, 2016~Day 35

I have faith in this week, which isn't something I often have. I'm going to change things; I feel like I have to. My confidence is dwindling and I honestly can't remember where it even came from, and I've been looking for any and every kind of distraction there possibly is. I've felt too mixed up lately, like there are no words to describe it. From questioning a million things to questioning myself. Not much else to say I guess...but most days are better than others I promise.

B-Tuesday, July 19th, 2016~Day 36

I am a rock
Uneasily defied
Lying to a rock is almost pointless
It can see through glass just like any other
But refuses to be swayed

Why bother with a lie that will only expose itself?
We're halves of a whole
Though a hole being driven through us is apparent
And there's no way to deny it any longer

If I'm in constant questioning
Is there room to call it quits?
I love her but I can't tell if she does me

If I value myself
Why spend what I have on something so worthless?

B-Wednesday, July 20th, 2016~Day 37

My feet are glued to the floor
And time's still ticking.
Oceans are still crashing
The sun still rises
And I watch it all.

I see it pass me by and wish for less than what I've been given
I can't hold onto the lies I tell myself
I need to let go of all of the falsehood
But I've seen too much hurt in the truth

I can't help but shield myself from now on
Hide myself from whatever tries to pop the bubble I'm enclosed in
I couldn't wish for better insight
Because it's not what I want
I just want to remain clouded in my 20/20 misperception

I should come clean but what good would that do?

B-Thursday, July 21st, 2016~Day 38

I dread what's coming
I'd looked forward with anticipation
But there's no telling what could happen
And nothing that ever happens ever happens well

One can only hope
Unless that one is me
And keeping your head down is easier than looking up
Or giving up comes too naturally

I have some left in the back of my mind
Who's to say
Maybe if I will it to be so
I'll actually have something to celebrate

G-Friday, July 22nd, 2016~Day 39

I had some worries but it all went as planned
I tasted sweetness
I basked in intense heat and comfort
I'd seen smiles I've missed for so long

I didn't realize how new today was to me
It completely slipped my mind
But once I opened up my eyes
I could see so many beautiful things

Colored lights outshining the moon
Laughing and silently wishing for attention
Wandering in the dark
But exploring what we've already seen
Learning what we already knew
And loving it over and over.

I can't wait to do it again.

R-Saturday, July 23rd, 2016~Day 40

I'd declared this week a good week. Tried to will it to be one, and it was fine until things I couldn't control seemed to get in the way. It kills me softly how I can feel guilt for someone else's discomfort with things that cannot be stopped especially when they constantly make requests they know they aren't happy with yet never learns. I can't let these things get to me, I refuse. I've been so comfortable lately I honestly will not allow a rotten apple to spoil that for me now.

G-Sunday, Sunday, July 24th, 2016~Day 41

I feel so indifferent
Tuning out lies with worries
Forcing my eyes open...

Time keeps running out on me
And the promises I make myself keep piling up
But somehow I get through okay every time
But there's no escaping the nag in the back of my mind
I can't tune her out can I?

There's no guarantee this can change
But I have to stay awake long enough to try

B-Monday, July 25th, 2016~Day 42

Today I ventured on my own
I wish I could've taken someone who wanted to voyage with me
Even on a journey as small as this one
But I wasn't good enough
And then I made mistakes
And I tried not to
But my best wasn't good enough

Even though I was chosen instead of someone better
I STILL didn't live up to my expectation
I never asked for anything to be expected of me, I hate such hypocritical presumptions
But if being held to impossible standards is the price I must pay for a bond like this
I'll be bankrupt in errors for quite some time

B-Tuesday, July 26th, 2016~ Day 43

I can feel the pressure of a new beginning
But it isn't a new chapter
Certainly unwritten for me

I didn't ask for her burden to be put on my shoulders
Nowhere is there room for what I need for me
And what they desire to no longer be bothered with

I can't force my smile anymore
Not with another set of eyes watching out for me
Especially now that I am so wanted.
I needed to be needed
But not like this

What I so wished for
Is being granted to punish me
And there isn't anything that can change it
I can't take it back
Or give myself a second chance

So I'm stuck in the beginning of my end

G-Wednesday, July 27th,2016~ Day 44

I've put myself in a torturous position
One I can't be cross about.

I declared myself heartless
Because with no heart there is nothing to break
But once someone
Anyone
Came along wishing for the slightest of access

I was at a loss

Nothing to lose
Nothing to gain
In the back of my mind the only person I want to restore my faith
Is constantly keeping me on a tightrope
But anytime they go to catch me
It's as if everything from before disappears
And that's a damn good feeling

R-Thursday, July 28th,2016~Day 45

I don't know why but this day feels really significant for some reason. There's been a LOT of change happening and that probably has a lot to do with feeling bad so lately, BUT I haven't had a 'dark' day in a while which makes me happier because I couldn't imagine trying to live day to day feeling like that. I've been having some dysphoria lately too but it's kind of come and gone dramatically in the last few days. I also got bad news so really nothing too great has been happening but hopefully a change of scenery and some reuniting with people I need will help. It's been a really shitty time but I haven't given up yet.

B-Friday, July 29th, 2016~Day 46

No heartbreak is greater than the ache felt from watching
Understanding.
Learning for once and for all that it doesn't always "take two"

Harsh words and undeserved hatred
Prolonging the tension and confusion in the atmosphere
With no reason to stay
No reason to make yourself the prisoner you envision
Why put yourself in a place of torment?
The happiness of others hasn't ever mattered before
So what's different?

If I were cruel
I'd say it was because power is nothing when the powerless are strong
Destruction is futile when there is nothing but broken pieces around

So a conjuring of a new victim is all you wish
Even if you loved them once
Fooled everyone into believing that you did no wrong
And causing the stress for so many others with no choice but to follow
the path you set out

A tyrant is always oblivious to their own tyranny
And you are no exception.

G-Saturday, July 30th, 2016~Day 47

I saw the rain a lot today
Sprinkled on windows
And dissolved in grass.

I saw a smile I've needed
And experienced a happy exhaustion
Tiny climbing hands
And squeaking laughter more musical than any symphony

I breathed in a welcome heat
And felt a cool breeze swarm my face

Like something from a book
Today was absent of faces
And filled with feelings

I couldn't tell you names because I can only remember words

A fan blowing warm air
A small round nose wrinkling from delight
A mouth open from a smile

Everything I needed right now

- Sunday, July 31st, 2016-Day 48

Heading back is a calm before the storm
If you know how bad the damage will be.

I'll take solace in today
In the quiet
Because before everyone can be on edge
There's still time to be normal
Time to appreciate the small memories made
Mourn over the tragedies this place has seen

But most of all to accept
That everything changes
And sometimes
Once in awhile
That change is good

B-Monday, August 1st, 2016~Day 49

My reality is changing
Had changed
Its not what I've expected
But I live with it no less

What am I supposed to do?
I can't change things
Will them to be different
I'll live with it in bitterness
Suffer in silence

My dreams will stay dreams
My wishes will drown in the bottom of fountains
I will remain burdened with a smile

Some things are taken with a grain of salt
I suppose this has to be too

But while I'll accept the changes that MUST happen
I long for the day change occurs where it is due

A morning when her evil will no longer rule
Cause any more pain to anymore people.

R-Tuesday, August 2nd, 2016~ Day 50

I moved, and I really think a change of scenery will improve things a lot, I think even for a little while it will, even though moving was extremely stressful. But this morning I woke up and peeked outside my window and saw a little boy's bike across the walkway, and a woman resting on the front steps. And two little boys and a little girl playing outside, and a tree right in the middle of all the apartments. And to the left there's a playground that I'm gonna take my nephew to. It's great, though living around more people is going to take getting used to. I hope nothing ruins this.

G-Wednesday, August 3rd, 2016~Day 51

I have so much faith in this place
So many possibilities
So many things that I Vision happening
It's only been a day and already I'm feeling better?
This must be a magical place
At least it must be if I'm actually trusting in it

I can't wait to really settle down
Sink my teeth in
Take hold of this place by the horns

I can tell that
After all this time
Any & everything that I've seen
Won't matter anymore
And if I had to ask for change
One final transition
I'm happy this could be it

B-Thursday, August 4th,2016~Day 52

Upon any realization comes stages of grief
Denial that what's happened has really been happening
I unknowingly became a piano and an audience
Not caring that he played for others to hear

It was almost like I ignored the sour notes
Because sometimes he'd play for only me
Even for a minute I was lost in the sounds

I never realized he was playing me for others
I was never to be his muse
Only his amusement
To play and pursue others with

And I let him.
Let him strum his guitar tuned with my heart strings
Allowed him, the magician, to blind me with card tricks
While he used me as his greatest trick
Magic words like 'I love you' cast every spell he needed
And it wasn't until he'd slipped up
Until someone else began to notice the hold he had

Until I'd asked to be clear
And he squinted his eyes to remember me
To ask what it was I wanted
But I couldn't say.

I wanted him
But a better him
I don't want him
But I always will
Somehow I'll find myself getting lost in his words
False or not
And somehow I'll pretend like I'm okay listening to him play me, the
piano

-Friday, August 5th, 2016~Day 53

Sweetness is swirled with fatigue
And bitter chocolate is a soft distraction
From soured thoughts
And spoiled mornings

And being busy is boring with a buzz
As if somehow going through the motions with laser focus
Is a drug of its own
Emptying your mind and still knowing everything
Quite an experience

And your best guess work
Turns out to be better than actual knowledge
What a power trip that is
That 30 seconds of an almighty limelight
Even though you're the only one who knows it's there

This is getting out of hand
The fame, all the fame
Inside your head
Your empty emotionless head
Is driving you a bit mad

But madness covered in chocolate is a good mix

D-Saturday, August 6th,2016~Day 54

My day started at 2 in the afternoon
And not once since then did I wake up
The darkest 90° I've ever seen.

I felt past the point of numbness
I was done
Am done
Daydreaming of balconies with loose rails
Broken staircases
Open bottles

I went so mad
You could call me a joker
But there was nothing funny about it
Wanting to die after loving life for so long
Is the most bittersweet feeling there is
And nothing could change it
The need for destruction is almost addicting

The need to tell others you want to be destroyed
Much less by yourself
Is not.
It is comforting to be able to hear the thoughts going through your mind
The impulses threatening
And do nothing.
Like doubting yourself actually comes in handy

You cannot challenge someone so empty
Especially not yourself
No matter the desire begging for action
There's no need in spilling from an empty glass
Especially if you can see through how empty it may be.

It was hard
Shedding half a tear
Needing to shed a thousand more
But you take what you can get
And I suppose this means it's not time to shed one

At least not yet

R-Sunday, August 7th, 2016~Day 55

Here goes. I hate this project. It's easy because it's a simple medium, but it's left me open to so many things, and has forced me to be honest with myself and that isn't something. I can't tell why or what's causing it, because there are so many factors, but my depression's all over the place lately and there's a possibility that it's worse which isn't comforting, but more answers would definitely clear things up and make me feel better. I've been feeling really dysphoric lately, more than normal, and I feel so horrible all day, like wanting to die or looking for some type of destruction that doesn't exist, and it just feels like I'm losing it somehow. I can't describe it, but confronting it every day means I actually have to deal with it and since doing so professionally isn't exactly an option yet I pretty much just close myself off. And I can tell that it's only making things harder.

D-Monday, August 8th, 2016~Day 56

Sleepless nights are expected now
The difficulty is in finding ways to spend them
I have the vast reaches any internet allows
Occupying myself with questions from strangers
But eventually everyone sleeps
And no one is left to distract me long enough to start any day

But I've noticed things that are so different.
How my smile hurts more than it used to
Or how my arms are constantly sore from keeping my elbows crooked
And how easy it is to act like everything's okay

But that's always been a talent of mine
So good it's almost magic now.

I can't channel it.
Make all of the pain into words and dialogue
Tell a story that's separate from mine
Though is mine all the same.

Maybe nothing is safe
I'm certainly not
The feelings of darkness
And desire to be destroyed

Man when did it get so bad?

G-Tuesday, August 9th, 2016~Day 57

I can feel it all fading away
Like layers of weight melting off

I got to hear my laugh ring again
Saw a better smile
And the need to drown is slowly fleeting
And it's not as hard to open my eyes

I just wish the people that helped me open them again
Weren't strangers
And the people that let me be blind
Didn't act as if they were.

That's the odd thing about dysphoria
No matter how much you want to close your eyes forever
It shows you those who wouldn't care if you did.

G-Wednesday, August 10th, 2016~Day 58

Its actually quite fascinating
How all of these colors and thoughts and voices and games
Take place in my head
Form puzzles with wooden pieces
Sometimes leaving splinters in their wake
All the fears and procrastination
All the time I wish I had

The wishes and hopes and dreams
No one can see inside
There's no way I can see
No way to tell what words or thoughts might come spilling out

A smile on my face
A plot in my head
A story being thought
Anger flowing through my veins, always so calm

No direction on my path
Uncertainty in my choice
No clarity in my fortune
And only a whisper in my voice

B-Thursday, August 11th, 2016~Day 59

I've found myself at a crossroads
Something so common
But this time it's different

This time I didn't jump out of the way
I faced it head on
And butt heads with someone else in the process

But I question how much they care about me
And I guess I offended
Rubbed salt in an invisible wound
And now we're at a silent face off

We can't wage war
Too many people would get hurt
Aside from us
Because it's much bigger than that

So many people will get hurt
It makes me wonder how we could ever coexist anyway
Two flames that could burn down an entire city in their wake

But here we are, colliding anyway

R-Friday, August 12th, 2016~Day 60

YIKES, I am NOT making things easier on myself. I've been sleeping more, and I don't want to die anymore but the whole episode made me irritable and looking back it was so easy to be ignored, I mean.... I hadn't slept in three days and I'd said pretty clearly that I wanted to die but oh well. I also may have lost someone that shouldn't have been found and don't exactly know how to feel about it.

B-Saturday, August 13th, 2016~ Day 61

I've looked into a magic mirror
And have seen what my future holds

And it isn't pretty
But I've sworn to take a different path
To change the pattern of behavior
Have put all this pressure on myself

But there's a certain beauty in creating your own expectations
Guess I just have to find it

G-Sunday, August 14th, 2016~Day 62

We've fixed what was broken
As if it never happened

I couldn't imagine my life different than it is now
Or how different it would have been.
How silent everything would be
How sad

I appreciate more that I let on
And say so little of what I want
But I know she won't forget
And I know she'll never stop caring
And that's something I'm glad to know.

G-Monday, August 15th, 2016~Day 63

I was beaten down in different kinds of heat
The heat of the sun
The heat of the moment
A cliché heat filled with passion

Passion.

Just fool's gold in this era
Convincing myself I care about what's beneath the surface
When all I want stares me in my face
Then my lips
Then my chest
And snaps back to attention at the snap of a ball

And I get to watch when the sun's heat gets too much and he almost
strips bare
And I catch myself staring
And him sighing at the sight of my hands
Carrying what he thirsts for in the sun's heat

But I can't help to wonder if he'd sigh the same
Knowing I thirst for him almost the same way
If he'd flash me a grin
Or help me as I passed by

If he'd show as much interest in me as he does for the game
It's all a game nonetheless
And I can't wait to find out who plays it better

G-Tuesday, August 16th, 2016~Day 64

Every ache is worth it
Every strain and sore muscle pushes me closer
And I know that it is going to pay off so much more than what I already
expect

And I get to watch it all from the sidelines
The nitty gritty work
The laughs
The strain

I can see everything up close
Feel the heat beating down like a challenge
I can't imagine this happening any other way
Even if it was by accident

R- Wednesday, August 17th,2016~Day 65

I'm very thankful for football managing, I love helping love what a great distraction it is. This week is ticking by slowly, but it never makes the days longer. It's made me feel okay for once.

B-Thursday, August 18th, 2016~Day 66

In the heat of the moment
The harshest of words speak the most truth

Fiery hate fueled by anger and pride
Even jealousy
Yet as soon as they're said you wish they weren't

You hope they weren't meant for you
Though you know you cannot deny
And the toxic realization makes you sicker
Since you know that you are worth more
And deserve so much better
But don't know where to find it

G-Friday, August 19th, 2016~Day 67

One final day of practice
Just a few final hours until we can rest
Not long until we can breathe easy and break from this new week

One last day under a hot sun
Few clouds
And the darkened skin to prove it
The striped lips to smile through it
And the sore legs to work for it

I almost can't wait for tomorrow
The excitement and laughs
The families and food
Soda and songs

All what football is about
And now I get my chance at a sideline

G-Saturday, August 20th, 2016~Day 68

I got my taste of action
My front row seat
Unprepared for what came next
But excited nonetheless

I regret not trying sooner
But I'd be lying if I said I didn't love every minute of it
Every huddle
Every helmet muffled conversation
Every drop of water that hit me

Every cheer and scream.
And when the lights came on?
That's how I knew it was real
How I figured it would continue to fill me with joy that I didn't think possible

And I'm ready for 10 more nights just like this

B-Sunday, August 21st, 2016~Day 69

The scariest things occur in my head
Like rollercoasters of thoughts
And wanting to be dead

My chest aches though hollow
My eyes hold back dreams
I just shake and wallow
While tearing at my seams

Roses are yellow
I try not to sleep
For dark thoughts and actions
May threaten to creep

R-Monday, August 22nd, 2016~Day 70

I'm not really okay I suppose. I'm fine, don't get me wrong, but I really hate this project. I take that back, I just hate life I suppose. It's nothing surprising, I'm just really very extremely unhappy, and it's a pity and a half that none of the happiness I have lasts very long. That's it I guess.

B-Tuesday, August 23rd, 2016~Day 71

I just want to matter.
I want to see past blurry staring
And frowned lips.
I want more than a heavy soul

I guess it's my soul I feel
It's felt too deep to be anything less
And my heart's been missing for longer than I recall

But it wants something I cannot give
Since I am not the one that's left my soul so heavy
I'm just the only one that cares enough to pick up the pieces.

And it wasn't until I had declared myself heartless
That everything within me replaced itself
Nothing so serious as sadness could be felt
Only a strong strain of disappointment

No caution about falling asleep
Since no number of hours is enough to fix me
And waking up in the same despair is harder with heartstrings attached

B-Wednesday, August 24th, 2016~Day 72

The panic sets in since time is running out
The one thing I told myself I had
Let myself believe for months I had such a luxury

Only I was losing it every minute
And that very thought rested in the back of my mind for so long
And now what?
I'll rush and race to finish what's barely started
Barely make it on time

Hope it passes for something
Hope it gets what it needs.
I can't think of a rouse to get out of this one
No lie comes to mind
So I'll just keep digging this hole I'm caught in
And hope I'll be able to climb out when the time comes

G-Thursday, August 25th, 2016~Day 73

The future is scary
Uncertain
Able to change at any given moment
But for now I'm flying

Speeding through the dark
The breeze
Twisting down unknown roads
And laughing at nothing!

Never have I ever felt so carefree
Never have I thrown caution to the night while feeling so secretly scared
Taking my own wheel couldn't feel better
And embracing darkness has never felt greater

G-Friday, August 26th, 2016~Day 74

One final play
A snap of a ball before another shot at proving we're worth the season
we were given
And I can't help but feel torn

Delighted to rest easy
Though not ready for this newfound action I've taken cover behind
And now that it's begun
It's already almost over

Just like everything else
New beginnings are always exciting
But the twinge of fear that sneaks itself into you so deep
Is hardest to get rid of
Even when you think you're ready
Always when you know you aren't

R-Saturday, August 27th, 2016~Day 75

This week has been pretty great, though my procrastination has set in fairly deep, and I've never been so excited about football, or almost anything really. My family is....... unchanged and indifferent, which isn't good, but is avoidable. I'm extremely excited for school to start, I feel like this year HAS to be a great year, and maybe I'll actually get things done. There are a lot of thoughts going through my head at times, but this week has been great for the most part, cheers to another one next week hopefully.

B-Sunday, August 28th, 2016~Day 76

I don't ask for much
Close to nothing, in fact
Having been seen as overreacting I guess I'll keep my disappointment
hidden

I've never been so angry over something so unimportant
No
It is important
Important to me
And I must remember that

That it's what I cared about
And no matter what else is said
That one thought kept me going
Gosh, I was so willing to sacrifice every other thing for this

Wait another week
Another two weeks
If it just meant having this one last time

G- Monday, August 29th, 2016~Day 77

I have not missed this
Early rising
Waiting for the sun to rise
Watching an invisible sky fill with color

Especially with all I have left to do
Still unfinished
Unsettled
But still I find myself excited
All of the people I've missed
The halls I haven't walked down
The stage I can once again walk across

The stories I have yet to tell
The adventures and wild things that will happen
I'll never admit it
But I'm going to miss this when it isn't mine to miss

G-Tuesday, August 30th, 2016~Day 77

I felt cold when I woke up
Everywhere
But cold with excitement
Anticipation

Everything fell into place for once
Everyone so familiar
Everything unchanged

And nothing keeping me quiet
I saw smiles I've missed
Hugged familiar bodies
Laughed about what hasn't happened yet

And today I realized
This place I'd come to love and hate
Was filled with what I needed
Love from people I loved
Who wasted no time in loving me right back

What I'd gone a long restless summer without
Was right back in my grasp
Was right where I'd never let go

G-Wednesday, August 31st, 2016~Day 79

If ever I ever wished for one thing
It would be to laugh in this chair
If I could spend every day waiting to sing
Life just wouldn't be fair

I walked in this room
My smile unreal
No impending doom
Can ruin how I feel

These bright dreadful faces
Old, new or unchanged
In silent sighted spaces
Waiting to be arranged

I've longed to hear
This piano play
The longing so near
For this sensational day

R-Thursday, September 1st, 2016~Day 80

I've never been excited to start school, especially not high school and ESPECIALLY not my last year. I've felt generally better since Tuesday (quite a change in just two days) because I've missed seeing my friends and teachers I that and for some reason I look forward to coming back every day. I have felt really good since I came to school, but of course here lies the eternal cloud of doubt and sadness that hangs over my head.

G- Friday, September 2nd, 2016~ Day 81

Underneath the lights
The thrill overpowers everything else
Still not real
I can't help but to feel like it is

The cold night
The countdown
Electrifying sunsets even though we can't watch them

These nights are nights I don't wish to quit
Nights I breathe
Even when we don't win

B-Saturday, September 3rd, 2016~Day 82

I'm not used to waking so happily
So light
Laying in stripes of sun and welcoming the warmth
Feeling ready about getting ready

I saw more colors than usual
And when I walked outside I could really feel the breeze.
I saw a plastic bag flying through the air
From rolling on the grass to soaring

And that was me
From so low to so high
So dreading to hopeful
And I can only wish she won't bring me down

Though she's already begun clouding my sun
Making me feel heavy again
Weighing me down
My hollow chest aching
My lids losing any motivation to stay open and look any longer

B-Sunday, September 4th, 2016~Day 83

I don't like dreaming
Always blurry
Always changing
And when I wake I feel like lead
Swimming to a surface of consciousness

Only to wake with the sun in my eyes
And confusion in my head
But for just a second I don't know where I am

Can't recognize my surroundings
But that means that for another night I've escaped
Gone to make believe places in my head
Not so scary when sleeping

And so gratifying when I'm awake again

D-Monday, September 5th, 2016~Day 84

There's no way
When I beg to be held
I am needing to be protected
I am pleading to feel safe
But I am wanting to be alone
So that I can feel alone
So I can think myself onto a ledge and make sense of what is happening

What IS happening?
Why is it happening to me?
Can anyone in the entire world make me understand?
I want to believe that I'll come back down every time
But I just can't.

Because one day I'll beg and I'll plead
But I won't say a word.
I will stay silent
And I'll wish that you came

And I'll think my way up
With no way to come down

R-Tuesday, September 6th, 2016~Day 85

Since school has started I've been more confident in my relationships, but I still feel like I have this cloud over my head, like sadness is lingering in the background whenever I seem to be enjoying myself. And it's so much harder to focus and I'm so incredibly unmotivated all the time, I kinda worry that it's going to get in the way of school and after school and I just really don't want it to ruin this year but it's already getting in the way.

G-Wednesday, September 7th, 2016~Day 86

For just a minute I can smile again
Surrounded by smiles and laughter
As inside jokes spill outward

Clutching my sides to steady myself
Singing duets with ten people
Dancing in a chair that I never want to get up from
There are no words

Only song!
And I can't help but sing along
And this feeling of mine
SO much better than fine
Feeling giddy all inside
Man, it's like heaven

B-Thursday, September 8th, 2016~Day 87

So great to be where familiarity is
It's a favorite word of mine
But the chaos is getting out of hand

YIKES

Flustered is the magic word
Feeling so excited but not how I'd hope
Fearing repetition
Though its imminent at this point

Having barely made it
Yet making it at all
Almost quitting
But sticking with it nonetheless

Y I K E S

G- Friday, September 9th, 2016~Day 88

I ran.
I mean actually ran
With the wind in my face
And my feet pounding the track
The field
The gravel

Just effortless running
My lungs not burning
Something so new
And loving it
Though I'd never admit I did

And the heat never got to me
Never caught up

And I danced?
No word stronger than danced I supposed
But it was such an amazing amount of joy
And flying and limited worries
Beautiful

G-Saturday, September 10th, 2016~Day 89

The morning after
And everything feels the same
And I can't feel anything in my legs
But my face still hurts from smiling

My sides are still sore from laughing
My eyes still blinded by the lights
And the light feeling still so present in my chest

And I know this is what I signed up for
This feeling
No clouds in my sky
No regret tinting my vision

No desire to quit
But if I get 12 more nights of this?
I'll never quit.

R-Sunday, September 11th, 2016~Day 90

90 days into this glorious project and I think I've realized what the problem is. I've suppressed my feelings and 'symptoms' for so long, and this project meant that I had to let them surface for this to even be possible. I do think I feel a lot more comfortable in a lot of aspects but since I have, I've definitely been so much more emotional than I'm used to, especially around other people, so I think that means it's working? I can't say for sure, but I think gradually not hesitating to say how I'm actually feeling is a big step towards really getting better.

G- Monday, September 12th, 2016~Day 91

So easy it is to lie in bright quiet

Too awake to sleep again
And too many wonders here to concentrate
Never very easy here
Nor anywhere

And now
Staring at the tasks I have before me
I should focus
Should give it all I've got
But it's too hard

All too much too fast
I don't know what I expected
But this can't be it

B-Tuesday, September 13th, 2016~ Day 92

Why are things falling apart so soon?
No matter how hard I try to control them
They spin out of hand

I'm not even paying attention anymore
Just going through the motions
Spinning in a deadly cycle
And still
Months to go before I figure out what this will do

G- Wednesday, September 14th, 2016~Day 93

I shouldn't be excited
Shouldn't feel relieved
But here I am
Celebrating what might be forever

Most would think him being here means I'm in danger
But I feel like this moment is long overdue
Another chance to breathe

Though I say I'll miss him
We both know I'm grateful

G-Thursday, September, 15th, 2016~Day 94

I'm flying
And soaring
And leaping
I'm roaring

Floating
Devoting
With no sugar coating

Gliding
I'm sliding
I surely don't mind and

While waiting
Degrading
These pills I'm fixating

Oops I've said too much

R-Friday, September 16th, 2016~Day 95

Tonight, I knelt for the first time in protest of black people being murdered. I felt scared, definitely, but not so scared that I abandoned my cause and stood again, but just enough to be worried about someone saying something to me directly. I've been feeling really angry and sad and getting high made me feel better, not quite happy, but lifted enough to be "content" with everything. And I still feel 'heavy' inside and don't feel like doing anything. AND I'M STILL SO UNMOTIVATED. 105 days left but you know what, still a work in progress.

G-Saturday, September 17th, 2016~Day 96

Wrapped in pounds of covers
Eyes glued to a screen for countless hours
Watching a world full of people who don't know me
But captivate me all the same

I talk to them
Laugh with them
Miss them
Like they're real
Like they aren't just from someone's imagination

But I get excited all the time nonetheless
Look forward to seeing them come on
Always hoping one day they'll pull me in with them

G-Sunday, September 18th, 2016~Day 97

Ceilings are so underrated
After a while if you look at them long enough
They have patterns
And your brain splashes them with colors

Like grainy movies
And blue paint rolling down walls

Colors on ceilings are more vibrant
Shapes so sharp
And as every hour ticks by
I feel no remorse for wasting my time

Though extreme dreading hangs over me
Crippling me with no longing to start another week on my feet

B-Monday, September 19th, 2016~Day 98

The sulking begins
Eyes glued to a phone instead of the floor
Emotions cooped under a hood

Perfecting a false smile
Convince anyone I'm okay
Just by blaming sleep

Sitting silently through a blurred day
And by now its caught on
That I'd rather ponder in silence

Though of course some might press
But I'll bend and not break
Never giving away any feelings
Because what are those anyway?

B-Tuesday, September 20th, 2016~Day 99

I have moved on from despair
Graduated from sadness to anger
And haven't moved on since then

And every day I swear I won't come back
Yet every next day here I am
Suffering in semi-silence

R-Wednesday, September 21st, 2016~Day 100

I'm halfway through. HALFWAY!! At this rate, I should be done by January, but I may continue this after I reach 200 because, despite how mixed my feelings are about this, I think it's actually gone pretty well so far. There are probably a lot worse days than good, but I am glad I did this because not only did I lock up my actual feelings, I also stopped writing poetry a while before this project kicked off. I resurrected the passion I had for writing, even though I haven't had much motivation for much else. I still have high hopes for this project as a whole; I hope it gives whoever reads them insight into my life with this illness or that someone else will know what I mean when they read these.

G-Thursday, September 22nd, 2016~Day 101

A little stress
Is less mess
No real worry
Or true hurry
I feel no tension to mention

Or a complaint in my mind.

I suppose I'm content
Kind of skating on thicker ice than normal
And gliding through this day because somewhere else someone just
came to life

Someone just took a big sigh
And looked so pleased with what they've done

And I can only wish that I become that happy too

G-Friday, September 23rd, 2016~Day 102

I won't remember this tomorrow
But it's what I'll never forget
Hands held tight
Words I didn't believe in this morning
Flowing shakily from my lips

But The tighter I squeeze
The more weight that drops from my shoulders
The less stress I feel
And when I say the names I forced myself to remember
The ones that will only be seen on gravestones
In hashtags

Tears threaten as I stand and brace for what is to come
But I'm surprised
I'm hugged and thanked
So many say that they are proud
That I am brave
And I feel as though I am

And I'm more ready than before
Ready to do it wherever and whenever
I am prepared
Despite the hollow sympathy
To face those who wish to silence me
To tell them that I will never stop speaking for those who have been
silenced

And I am never going to quit

G-Saturday, September 24th, 2016~Day 103

Tonight was a big dark room and heat
Tonight was feeling music before hearing it
Tonight was feeling parts of him I'd hoped for
And tonight will never leave me

It was bending and swaying
It was grooving with bodies next to mine
It was him laughing in my ear
Him guiding me with his arms
It was me laughing too hard to move

I sat under a red lamp
I savored every laugh that escaped me
I saw more than what was there
But I cherished it all the same

I smiled the whole night
I smiled through the dancing
I smiled through the dinner
And every song that played on the radio
Retold the story of tonight

G-Sunday, September 25th, 2016~Day 104

Glitter covers sleepless bags
Like blankets on bare legs

But since I'm up at dawn
With my smile still raw from last night
I can live with a "morning after"

Especially after seeing such a wide smile
On such a deserving child's face

R-Monday, September 26th, 2016~Day 105

Since friday, which was very successful, I've felt SO much better. I had an exhilarating time at homecoming, though I am really trying not to let any feelings get in the way of everything. BUT I've been having a much better time than last week in general, and I'm considerably less angry than before. AND THERE ARE 95 DAYS LEFT HOLY MOLY

G- Tuesday, September 27th, 2016~Day 106

I asked for rain
And I got it
I got rain
And wind
And I huddled through a hustle

And I laughed despite the frigid winds
And I'd began to dislike rain
Which has always been a comfort me

So even though I laugh and open wide to taste the raindrops
I wonder if this means things I've loved
Just don't last

G-Wednesday, September 28th, 2016~Day 107

Sudden surprises
Planned but still progressed
Are always so pleasing

I can't say for sure
But there's just something so gratifying
So mind easing
About life actually going your way

B-Thursday, September 29th, 2016~Day 108

Just one day left in this week
A smile painted across my face
Since the dread in my heart is so so obvious

I've been ready for this week to end for so long
Oh sorry
I've been ready for this *year to end for so long
Scratch that
*Life

I'm only here for the small things
The delayed deadlines
The successful presentations
The sing along every other lifetime
But in between them is what I'm "supposed" to do
What I "must" complete
What is expected of me?

But all I need is the victories
All the success
All the time

G- Friday, September 30th, 2016~Day 109

Damn it feels good to be back
In this chair I always claimed as my own
With the family I really care about

Four years and I still feel so light around them
Day 2 and I still smile at their voices
And nothing has changed for worse
Nothing so different we can't move on together

And in this chair with this movie we've seen a dozen times
I'd trade nothing and no one to be with them for four more

R-Saturday, October 1st, 2016~Day 110

I find myself experiencing "symptoms"? I don't know, that's a pretty strong word if you ask me, it's more like minor setbacks, they come with the Depression Package™ just bitter pills to swallow really. There's no telling what I'd do if these were a real problem. I just need an extra push getting out of bed, and a BIG extra push to actually get things done. I can't really concentrate, and my will to live hasn't been too high in numbers. I don't want to say that this project isn't helping because, despite any records, I think it is, it's a great outlet for me to say what I want/need to say without judgement or (much) filter and I sometimes even look forward to doing it every day. And it's not a waste and I don't even care about whether or not anyone sees this. I don't know, maybe it's irrelevant, but it's like every time I type I'm a little less angry/sad/whatever. Yay for that.

G- Sunday, October 2nd, 2016~Day 111

It's the sunniest days that go noticed
Because they're somehow discomforting
But only because they're too much

"Too" bright
"Too" Warm
"Too" anything

And I know people like that
Never appreciated for their sunlight
And I wish I could tell them
Each of them
That they shine so bright in my life

`B-Monday, October 3rd, 2016~Day 112

I never want to be here
Too bright too early
And so much still to do

But everything I do
When I sit myself to start
Every nerve flairs

And there isn't anything at ease
Especially myself
As I sit
Or stand
Or move

And nothing happens
No progress is made without pain
Nothing goes restlessly
And everything is somehow at risk

B-Tuesday, October 4th, 2016~Day 113

Today I lay in this bed
And I don't move
Won't move
This thing that I've made up for good reason
Has somehow become real

Become plausible

I know I should tough it out
These days aren't long ones
But I just can't

Can't

That's been such a prominent word of mine lately
I mean I'm even starting to believe it

D-Wednesday, October 5th, 2016~Day 114

I've been asking myself the same question
'How did I let it get this bad?'
Every day was like having my arms tied behind me
Watching myself struggle for clarity

Every experience so uncomfortable
So tiring
Everything an out of body experience
Until there was rarely a moment I didn't wish for death
Not so immediate
But not entirely undesired

R-Thursday, October 6th, 2016~Day 115

It's 11 pm right now and I have just finished the rough draft for the background research paper as a part of this very project. I HAVE NEVER FELT SO RELIEVED. I am still behind on other things for sure, but I cannot express how much weight is off of my shoulders. And this weekend I can celebrate another year alive along with a newfound desire to live.

I am empowered.
I know what I am
What I fight for
Who I am fighting for

I know that while I will not stand
I will never stand down
And I will not cower in fear of those who don't know

I will rise when I am pushed
I will speak
I will smile
I will remember.

Because they forget
They forget that this skin cannot wash off at the end of these
troublesome days
This skin I'm in is for forever
And while you can go home
To your tailored world
I must bow my head and be grateful
And for what?
For not being killed?
For 'getting' to live?

This is not what I was meant to stand for
So I will not stand.
I will kneel and remember
I will kneel and respect
I will be proud
And I will never surrender

G-Saturday, October 8th, 2016~Day 117

Heat passes through my lips
Ever so subtly
And the slow rise of my chest is not new to me
But it's no habit either

From a wall's eyes
It would seem like something from an old movie

A black kitchen chair
On a dingy kitchen floor
With a dim light to keep my eyes low

And the hum of a fan against my leg
As puffs of smoke swim higher in the air

My nerves may dissolve
But this smile is sure to stick with me until morning

G-Sunday, October 9th, 2016~Day 118

I rarely thought I'd get to see this day
A birthday.

And that's all there is to it
Today
Yesterday
Friday
All so full of light
Everything assuring me that still breathing for this long was worth it

And now I know that it was

G-Monday, October 10th, 2016~Day 119

The best birthday I have ever had.

This was the best celebration of mine
Of course it's one of the few I've ever had

But it was filled with sweet wishes
And warms faces
And cloudless feelings

And I felt beautiful in every single way
And I felt loved like I've never known

And there's absolutely no way to convince me
That this birthday could be beat.

R-Tuesday, October 11th, 2016~Day 120

This past weekend I was fortunate enough to celebrate my birthday, the best one I've ever had, and I can honestly say that with no exaggeration. I felt so incredibly happy and loved, and it's exactly what I needed after a string of bad days. I even wrote a little! I can only hope I have more days like these to come.

G-Wednesday, October 12th, 2016~Day 121

I can't help but stir when consumed by this feeling
Stronger than happiness
Tamer than excitement
When I walk through the halls I'm confined to
And see such beautiful faces covered in smiles
And even the ones in frowns

Because I love them
I love them all
And no matter how they see the world these days
I can only be sure that they feel the same

G-Thursday, October 13th, 2016~Day 122

All I can feel is the music in my chest
From my voice
From the beat humming in my throat
And in here I can stare across the room

And see nothing strange
And we all laugh in the face of rules
Like a family
Like we're a real kind of family

G-Friday, October 14th, 2016~Day 123

I must admit
I imagined this night with less laughter
And more subsurface touches
More sideways glances
Less talking
More showing

I'd hoped for line crossing
And secretive exploration

But for now I'll settle
For big smiles
And puns around a foreign dinner table
And jokes in the parking lot that make my head spin

Even with a let down
I guess I've won happiness

G-Saturday, October 15th, 2016~Day 124

Iced coffees
And leafless fall mornings
With frosted breezes
And bumpy rides

The morning is warmer than usual
And we'd been warned to stay inside
But there wasn't anything that could make me stray from the light
feeling I carried

From an early morning
Filled with biscuits and sweetness
To a victorious afternoon
And a blissfully quiet day

And though I knew today has to end
I smiled anyway

R- Sunday, October 16th, 2016~Day 125

This week has been oddly yet consistently great, and I am definitely convinced that it's only because of my friends. I don't know why it took so much sadness to really appreciate them, but nonetheless I am eternally grateful to all of them. I also haven't written in such a long time (besides this) and it's killing me softly, but hopefully I'll conjure up some time...

G-Monday, October 17th, 2016~Day 126

I never noticed how many colors these walls held
Inside and out
But so much is noticed when you keep yourself from looking
Holding your eyes to the same floor

And though I never want to be here
I look forward to looking at the same large windows
Sealed with irony
And hope that one day I won't get caught being so coy

But there's such a thrill in almost getting caught
Especially when there's no rhyme or reason to play such a game
Well
At least not without feelings

D-Tuesday, October 18th, 2016~Day 127

I haven't felt an anchor this heavy in a bit
Haven't been dragged so far down in a while
And people are trying to pull me back up
But I just stare at the water from beneath the surface

Floating
Waiting to be swallowed whole

I don't know why I thought this might have been a good idea
To stay in this place and settle for slight sleep
Knowing that this place isn't for me
And never has been

Just sitting in a room filled with light
And only seeing the dark corner across the hall
Remembering that secret on a shelf
Hidden so well

And even though I'm sinking slowly
I find myself pulling it out
Popping it in
Floating up with the anchor still stuck to me

B-Wednesday, October 19th, 2016~Day 128

The morning after is always hard
Like you've got a cold
But you've washed your face and braved it out

Like you didn't spend the night closing your thoughts with medicine
cabinets
Like everything is okay
Like you didn't weigh 600 pounds when you got out of bed this morning

It's hard
And impossible
But somehow you keep doing it every time
And the carousel never stops turning

B-Thursday, October 20th, 2016~Day 129

I keep flashing back to that night.
Tears in a dark room
Noiselessly landing on a soft floor
Eyes wide with nothing to see

Even as I laugh now
Sigh with a present happiness
Even though my flashes of the past keep threatening

And it isn't as if my desire to live is restored
At least not entirely
I am more grateful for these moments
But then again
I'm used to being grateful

R-Friday, October 21st, 2016~Day 130

This week has been exceptionally bad. Well, dark is more like it, but oh well. I can't describe how disappointed I feel that this has happened again, especially considering how good I thought I'd been doing. It's just a sinking feeling really, but I don't know what I'm more disappointed about; not going through with it or wanting to in the first place. Also, I keep promising myself that I'll write more but that's not happening anytime soon.

G-Saturday. October 22nd, 2016~Day 131

And I woke up the next morning
I opened my eyes from their game night haze
Turn from the sickly heat pulsing through the window
And feel for the sheets around me

And I let down my hair
And stretch into reality

And I see what I left alone
What people have decided to say
And I feel like living again
So I capture the moment through a morning lens
Then leave it to chance once again

G-Sunday, October 23rd, 2016~Day 132

The only way to bring it up
To let everyone else know

"What's wrong?"
"What's going on?"

To answer the questions

"Are you okay?"
"Do you need anything?"
"Are you sure?"

Is to pretend that you're okay with not being okay
And to laugh to keep from crying
And to hope that they catch on
But most importantly
Breathe when they finally do

G-Monday, October 24th, 2016~Day 133

I finally caught a sunset
A surreal sky that seems to get away from me all the time
One that only appears for other people
But I finally caught a glimpse

While sitting in the cold
While waiting
I got to see one for the first time

So maybe everything will be okay

G-Tuesday, October 25th, 2016~Day 134

I keep seeing reminders of what love is
In kisses and hugs
And nowhere near me do I find it

I remind myself that it's not what I want
No matter how hard I've tried to force it
There just isn't the same heart beating in my chest

It doesn't quickly beat
Does not skip
Has not fluttered in quite some time

But here I am
Holding my breath
Running in circles

Just so I can feel it again
The breathless pace between my lungs
The sprint of my stomach

Some level of feeling other than one sided attraction
And impatience for non-answers

Maybe I'm not heartless
But maybe my heart just hasn't fully grown back yet

R-Wednesday, October 26th, 2016~135

I don't know what it is, but it feels like I'm in a constant battle between being okay to barely making it sometimes. It is something I need to see someone about but I've been saying that for a while and to be honest I don't know what I'd say at this point. On the other hand, I think that I'll continue this past the 200-day mark. I don't know if anyone will actually read the reflections, but if you are, know that I love this project more than I let on, I promise :)

G- Thursday, October 27th, 2016~Day 136

It was just another Thursday
But it was a football practice Thursday
A cold football practice Thursday

Nonetheless another Thursday
Where we acted as if it were the first Thursday
How we behaved like it was our last Thursday

How we talked like it was Friday
Why we hustled like it was Wednesday
When we laid back like it was Monday

How we spent every day of the week
Simply in Thursday
But not just any Thursday
Just another one

G- Friday, October 28th, 2016~Day 137

Tonight I painted my lips black
And I stood
For those who stood in front of me
As opposed to kneeling
For those who lie restlessly under me

And I was torn for a great deal
But it came down to when
The soldier I saw in the mirror that day
Did not compare to those in front

But that is not one comparison
For no nations share my belief
Believe in my honor
Validates my voice

And no nation
Has let me down as much as the one I stand upon

G-Saturday, October 29th, 2016~Day 138

And I laid eyes on her
And I smiled though we both said nothing
Yet nothing needed to be said

After so many years of completing thoughts
And relaying arguments
What is there to say?

And after weeks of silence
Of distance
There isn't much to speak about
But more than enough to catch up on

So we joke
And play
And act as if we aren't growing apart
And we drive around
Just this once
And when I leave again
We'll be back here in a few months
And repeat it all again

G-Sunday, October 30th, 2016~Day 139

Goodbyes aren't hard
When hellos are so insincere
Not that we won't be missed by one another
But
Well

There was no reason to miss anyone

And now plain as day
I wear the sacrifice so clear on my face
My glasses snapped in two
Patched poorly to allow me to see if only for a while

Because I was already blind to what needed to be said
And now I am forced to try and see how to face it
How to unblur the lines between reality

And I suppose now it cannot go ignored
Something like this always comes to surface
And though now we have to split apart again
It won't matter how clearly I am able to see

R-Monday, October 31st, 2016~Day 140

Today showed me that I jump straight to wanting to die whenever I feel attacked by anything. I'm fine now of course, but I'm always ready to completely give up when things get tough. When did I become so weak? When did I become so ready to stop trying? Why did it get so bad so soon? Can I make it stop?

G-Tuesday, November 1st, 2016~Day 141

I was supposed to be watching nature
Half bloomed November flowers
Vacant fountains
But instead I chose paths

Pictured all the roads they'd lead to
Captured their cut off trails
Disappearing guidelines

I didn't even notice until I was home
All the flowers in photos were undoubtedly beautiful
But seeing those paths a second and third time made me wonder
Why did they look so different?

After I couldn't cross them anymore
After they didn't lead me to novel worthy pavements covered in
hardened leaves
I obviously didn't see them until I left
It's clear that I took pictures so I wouldn't forget

I just wish I remembered more now

Yesterday I pet a cat

It's that simple
I pet a cat

It was the first cat that I'd pet in a long time
And I needed it
This strange cat that lived among gardens
So content and stone faced sitting by my knee
And I felt the same
Although I'd only ran into it by accident
I stopped to let it curl beside me in the cold

And I felt sad
Because it's getting cold out here
And this isn't any cat of mine
So it shouldn't be any worry of mine either

But it's purrs rumbled under my fingertips
And it never stopped scowling at me
But I worried
And cared
And felt like this cat was mine to protect
But I couldn't

So I ended up leaving
And I'm still wondering if it's okay
In those gardens
In the cold

And I realize that even though i just pet a cat

I'm seeing that it was all I needed to care again

B-Thursday, November 3rd, 2016~Day 143

Why take myself seriously anymore
Why make anyone worry
Why cause a panic when I can laugh it off?

I'm just a small buzz in a swarm of sad bees
With no one problem to stand out

No progress made
Granted new sight yet still unable to see a solution
And I'll blame myself
And sit in a puddle of pity
Until I'm all out of laughs

G- November 4th, 2016~Day 144

It's senior night
So everyone is standing with their parents
Roses in hand
And excitement in their eyes

And names are being called so we can walk forward under the lights
Our walk of fame
Our 15 seconds to matter

And I'm standing in between two people who aren't my parents
But matter to me
And parts of me feel vacant since I'm not taking the same walk as
everyone else
But I take pride in knowing I can walk with freed shoulders
With no fear of being caught in an explosion between the two

And as I'm walking down the field
My hopes and favorite memories shouted out above me
I stare into the smiles of the friends I've made
Almost not believing that this means it's almost over

R- Saturday, November 5th, 2016~Day 145

Nights like that are always bittersweet because they fuel my longing for things to be different. Last night I felt happiness and awkwardness and sadness all at once, and the game was great and seeing so many of my friends, but I feel like every game is a distraction and when I leave, my high dissolves and I'm still missing something. And a lot of the time I feel like all of my good days come from distractions because there's always some kind of underlying sadness waiting.

B- Sunday, November 6th, 2016~Day 146

Just 3 days till damnation
All anyone can even talk about
And I'm laughing about it
And joking around it
But I'm praying for a close way out

There's faith and there's disbelief
Apparently two sides to this tragedy
A right and a wrong for those of us underneath
Left in some unknown form of grief

I can laugh now
And shadow my worry
While I stress here helpless
Unable to do anything but hope it'll hurry

B-Monday, November 7th, 2016~Day 147

There are promises all around me
To shelter in place of fear
To leave behind their lives
Pray to darkening skies
And say goodbyes to ones they hold dear

I offer a strong smile
Hope it makes up for miles
With no comfort to give
Since even I'm afraid to live
And nothing is sure any longer

I can only sit and wait
For a sign that maybe we'll be okay
But this isn't our game
No matter how much we think we play

B-Tuesday, November 8th, 2016~Day 148

It's quiet everywhere today
Everyone's on edge about the task at hand
Worried to keep our hopes to ourselves
And I'm no stranger to cautious discretion

But I have to know
Need an answer to who I can trust
And it's gonna drive me crazy
But all I can hope
Is for a drop of mercy

I don't want to wake to this world tomorrow
I don't think I could handle waking upside down
Back in time
Watching my back twice more
As if everyone's an enemy

Even though they just might be

D- Wednesday, November 9th, 2016~Day 149

I've spent a lot of my life awake at 3 a.m.
But none have been quite like this

I was terrified of this
Hopeful that my future would survive
That my life could hold on a few more years
I counted everything I felt this morning

How many times I forgot to blink
How many tears slid down my cheek
The number of rapid rise and falls of my chest
How did this happen?
How did we let it?
I won't move from this spot today
I won't face what will happen yet
I can't

I don't know what's supposed to happen now
But I hope they're all happy
They wanted this
They chose this
Over faulty trust
And I could die tomorrow
Vanish from this place meant to be my home
But god, do I hope they're happy

R-Thursday, November 10th, 2016~Day 150

One of my worst fears came true at such an odd hour, and I barely slept,
barely felt anything other than fear and sadness. And I sat at home,
nothing possibly motivating me to move from this spot. I don't
understand how this could have happened or what will happen next.
This makes enough sense I guess, since it isn't everyone's lives are at
risk. I don't know what the future could hold or how it could ever look
up. Oh well, maybe life isn't worth its marbles if something like this
could happen.

B-Friday, November 11th, 2016~Day 151

I missed his birthday
And I would've said something
But I wasn't sure
Even though I should've been
I doubted myself
After years of being certain

But it was easier then
All it took was one phone call
I didn't have to sulk in fresh abandonment
I could shrug off the guilt of 364 other silent days
But now it's been days
And a birthday
There's no guilt

Just a new emptiness
Covered with uncertainty
And laid to rest

I can't make the decision
It's out of my reach
But he'll talk to me somehow
He always finds a way

G- Saturday, November 12th, 2016~Day 152

Even if I'm not one to sleep
I can fake my way through any rise
And today was conjured from the blinks of sleep
But I remember today

Cold skin so early in the morning
Aching cheeks from the stretch of one hundred grins
My least favorite game
But the only time we were really a team

Sweetness I never knew existed
Honey butter and how sweet it tasted
Honey butter and how much I love saying it
Honey butter and how sensible it felt dripping down my chin
More tastes
More laughs

And the smell that always takes me back
To when I was more than visiting
To when guilt trumped satisfaction
And every surface made my gown stick to me

All this raced through my mind
All this before 9 p.m.

Sunday, November 13th, 2016~Day 153

I guess I'm still in disbelief
And holding a visible grudge
But fear and determination stand as my Trojan horse
Anger waiting patiently inside
Even though it's not a strong facade

And I'm finding out so much about everyone around me
Who I wouldn't have thought to care
Who I'd hoped was fighting by me

So odd
Watching this twilight zone fold out around me
Laying warning that I will not be moved
While watching the impossible prove me wrong at the same time

G-Monday, November 14th, 2016~Day 154

Here I was
Another sleepless night
Not so sleepless
More like sleep fought

But I don't look forward to today
Since it's still considered night
I can lay and think for once
Not so dangerous around now
While my head is too thick to move
My eyes heavy and stubborn

And I think today will be floated
Glided through with no recollection
Damn I've never hated Mondays so much

R- Tuesday, November 15th, 2016~Day 155

The past few days have kind of trickled along, and I'm still in disbelief at
it all. And I feel like everything I felt in July is going to come back. It's
been weird trying to act as if everything is normal, even though I'm
more than grateful to have friends that are understanding about it all
and feel the same way because I don't know what I'd do if I was the only
one afraid.

B- Wednesday, November 16th, 2016~Day 156

In a day I've convinced myself
That I'm all alone again
So I turn myself away from any confrontation

And I've withdrawn again
So I turn away from my mirror
And project smiles to those in need
Ignoring the absence of mine
But what else is there to do?

I'm not necessary to me
And there isn't much room left in this world
Not for this many frowns
So if I can't change mine
I might as well accept it

G-Thursday, November 17th, 2016~Day 157

Sometime things never end up how I wish they did
Well more than sometimes
A lot of sometimes

But something somehow some way comes along
Trying to get me to remember something worth it
Which is a bit cynical if you ask me
Because I don't understand
How am I supposed to be knocked down?
Then picked up again

And be okay?

I can remember why I'm ever happy
But I know I'll never forget why I'm not
And something about that is comforting
Grounding

So I know I won't float away in the sadness
I'll swim
And I'll live

G- Friday, November 18th, 2016~Day 158

I'm not one for breakthroughs in theaters
Or an epiphany in a verse
But tonight was something else

It made me question if anything is worth it
And this time I mean it
I wondered if this means there's something beyond pencil pushing
I think back a lot on my own
But now I know to not just think
But to remember

And I remember all of the pointless things in my past
Pointless tears
Pointless fights
Pointless upsets
Meaningless everything.

And I remember times where I knew it was pointless
And I knew that later it wouldn't matter
But I would tell myself that in the moment it was the most important
thing to me

And I guess I was living in the moment
But forgetting the future
I was doing it all wrong
And tonight reminded me that I have more chances
Almost infinite chances
To remember correctly
And live right

B- Saturday, November 19th, 2016~Day 159

It's been nonstop challenges
What they call 'obstacles'
Full on hurdles to jump over

As if every good has to come with ten bads
And there can't be any sun without hours of rain to follow
And all the fuss I've made before is coming back around

It's some unforeseen and unnecessary pattern
Unpleasant
Unwanted
Unhappy

I'm unhappy
Always
So
Unhappy

R-Sunday, November 20th, 2016~Day 160

Nothing's been looking up for a while, and everything seems as if it's going to keep downhill for some reason. I am actually hopeful, with every break there's some relief so I hope this time around I'll get to breathe a little before I implode with all of these things scattering my brain.

G-Monday, November 21st, 2016~Day 161

And somehow
Sunlight prevails
Just as the last time
And the time before

And I can see and bask in it's warmth
And breathe before the storm starts back up again

I don't have to live in the dark
But it's so much quieter there
But no one ever lived quietly

G-Tuesday, November 22nd, 2016~Day 162

Today wasn't as awful
Didn't kill me quite as much
Today left me breathing

And I'm genuinely hopeful this time
Like the last time
And the time before
Because this month is almost over
The fastest uneventful air of it all
Finally coming to a close

So maybe I can look on
Look up
Focus on what really matters
And leave all of this heartache behind

G-Wednesday, November 23rd, 2016~Day 163

Seeing everyone's lives pan out for the best
Watching and waiting while they live
And make me glad to

While everyone gets what they deserve
And wait for my chance to get there too.
I may be unsure of how I'll get there
But I know where to start

I'll prop myself up
Turn up the background noise
And make something happen
Catch up what I've been missing

And maybe I won't miss so much next time

G-Thursday, November 24th, 2016~Day 164

I just felt so damn good today
It began on actual fire
But didn't burn too much
And it left me with more than nothing for a change
So how bad could it be when I look back?

I don't surround myself with them usually
But today I'm glad I did
I felt like we made sense
Like we weren't pretending this time

And I lived in an autumn haze
And responsibility was a stranger
And laughter found me again
And I really wish this was the last day
If it was a last day
I'd gladly live it again

R-Friday, November 25th, 2016~Day 165

This month has been long, and I feel like with the amount of bad days I've been having maybe something isn't working. Or I've just been in a rut for the last 25 days and I can't really climb out. I feel like I'm just breathing a little more each time and if that's not frustrating then maybe it won't ever really look up after all. I'm still hopeful of course; if this month is ending then the next has to be amazing, it has to be.

G-Sunday, November 27th, 2016~Day 166

I don't like myself like this
Fluttering at text message
Face flushed
Giddy through every other moment of the day

But here I am again
Met with someone's piqued interest
Me
Who went untrying
Who did nothing
Caught the attention of whom I swore was just a fantasy in my head

But I guess it's not
She says that she means it
And maybe she does

I think it'll be a good fit
At least for now
Since it's brand new
Untouched

I know I shouldn't be
But I'm excited
Excited and hopeful
A dangerous combination

Because if this is anything like last time
It'll simmer and turn flat
Or burst in flames
But for now I'll enjoy the heat

B-Monday, November 28th, 2016~Day 167

And just like that
Life's back to terrible

I'm back to giving up
Back to not loving
Back to not trusting

Because I always get my hopes up
And I'm let back down
So I don't know what this means
But I know for sure that if it lasts as long as it has
Then I won't make it

G-Tuesday, November 29th, 2016~Day 168

I guess I've got to remind myself
Of what I've got to do
Because if it's not right in front of my face
I won't ever believe it exists

I've put my priorities on pause for some reason
Because I've let myself run ragged
And I'm still counting down to the days
Since there's only one more to go

Hope has been the word of the month
For some reason I keep losing it
And though I find it again every time
I wish it would stop leaving

But yeah
Once again I'm hopeful

G-Wednesday, November 30th, 2016~Day 169

I'm terrified of heights
Afraid of dropping low
Scared I'll lose my grip
And that whatever poor tower I'm in
Will crumble right beneath my feet

I've opened my eyes again
I've walked ten steps closer to my goal
And I promise that I won't stop now
I'll hash it out
Swear to go down kicking
I'm terrified of heights
But I like this view from the top

R-Thursday, December 1st, 2016~Day 170

Okay there's a definite pattern here. Every up has a down but there's
nothing in that saying to indicate that the down has to plummet me into
the negatives or that it absolutely must happen immediately after I dig
myself out of the trenches. 30 days left. Lots of discovery but little
improvement.

B-Friday, December 2nd, 2016~Day 171

I should feel broken again
But it's the "again" tripping me up
I should be more upset
More anything really

I don't know what this brings the tally to
I never kept count if I'm being honest
I've never felt the need

I don't feel any new emptiness
The same hollow remains unfilled
And only something like this could remind me of it

I doubt he'll come back again
But I know some naive part of me is going to keep hoping
Keep wishing

Deep down I'm glad
He didn't deserve what he was getting
But I wish I knew
Because he swore

Swore that he wasn't running away
That he'd stick around
But it just hurts most that the one time he broke it
He didn't give me any warning

G-Saturday, December 3rd, 2016~Day 172

It doesn't quite feel like December
But it gladly isn't November any longer

I rose early
Wandered aimlessly down aromatic aisles
And felt a warm sun and a forgiving breeze

And I indulged in old habits
Got to taste sweet taboo
Even though surprisingly it was not enough
And I thankfully tapped out

I meant to focus today
But I'm not complaining at all

G--Sunday, December 4th, 2016~Day 173

I've stretched out the day

I've made the day longer
Covered the sun with a red sheet corner to corner
To block and light from screeching my way

Because every shine brings with it a haze
I no longer have to fuss over nonsense
At least for now
With a red cloth pulled corner to corner
The sunlight removed from disturbing my focus

But streaks creeping through carry with them a dulling glare
And my aching shoulders are fresh with stress
Because my body knows when I'm trying
And it's already starting to give up

So I can only hope to stay in the dark
And pay attention for once
So I don't sink behind

B-Monday, December 5th, 2016~Day 174

I think I aim too high
Under all of my complaints is wishful thinking
And my Optimism clouded with doubt

And this morning I thought I was doing alright
Looked on the bright side
Had a laugh at life's mishap

And it still turned me around
And threw me flat on my ass

R- Tuesday, December 6th, 2016~Day 175

I'm spiraling again. After another short hand was dealt to me I tried to keep hope and tried to do better but I'm definitely going downhill from here and I don't know how to stop and I'm not sure how to quit but guess I'll find some way out of this too right?

G-Wednesday, December 7th, 2016~Day 176

Indifference is a special gift
Not quite careless
Not so neurotic to warrant discomfort

I can just sit while my mind unravels
While all of my marbles slowly lose themselves

I can sit here and say again and again
How I will do what I swore to do
And how this time I really do mean it

But I know that as much as I want to believe myself
I'll just lay back and wait for it to all fall apart

G-Thursday, December 8th, 2016~Day 177

I can't say I'm lucky
But I get pretty darn close

I've woken up too soon to feel
Since sleep is such a dangerous game
I run the risk of forgetting more each time
But I wouldn't forget this

I'm softer again
Newer
Like I've been born all over again
But just my body
And nothing more

I guess something like this isn't always good
It's ill-advised for some reason
But that doesn't mean I'll let it stop me
Come on, when have I ever

G-Friday, December 9th, 2016~Day 178

I love to talk to strangers
They've become some of the best people in my life

I could talk for hours about anything
Tell countless stories they haven't heard
And listen to all of theirs

I don't worry that they'll leave me
Or hurt me
Or lie to me
Why would they?
They don't owe me anything
And they're too far to make a difference either way

So yeah I'd say it's a fair trade
Some of my best friends were strangers
But there's nothing strange about that

When you think about it
Its quite ironic
We're warned that strangers would hurt us
That they were unsafe
And now they're some of the most necessary people in my life
Ain't that strange

B-Saturday, December 10th, 2016~Day 179

The monster is back
Its ugly head is bigger and turning just as much
Trembling in disapproval
Just waiting to knock me down and bury me

I wish it would
I'm sick of looking at myself
Looking in mirrors and store windows as if there's something worth
seeing
I hate it
I hate me

I don't know if it's wrong or bad to feel this way
But I don't care this time
I'm back to hating myself folks
A whopping amount of time went by before nature ran its course

This is only destined
I can't be happy if I'm not even worth looking
What sense would that make?
I couldn't stretch a smile if I tried
But why would I even bother

R-Sunday, December 11th, 2016~Day 180

I've been reduced to low self-esteem. 10/10 a great time happening right about now for me. But I am seeing my friends trying, and I am paying attention, and I do appreciate it but it's all buried behind doubt and blah blah blah. I'm tired of singing this song and trotting through this dance but I step up to the stage every single time.

D-Monday, December 12th, 2016~Day 181

I almost didn't today
I really almost didn't.

I just couldn't.
I was paralyzed this morning
Couldn't
Didn't
Get out of bed for a long time

But I made it
Because I have to
If it wasn't for 'have to' I'd probably be there now
And I'd stay there tomorrow
And no one could tell me that I needed to do any different

B-Tuesday, December 13th, 2016~Day 182

You know that nagging voice in your head?
Well mine is much different

She's not in my head
She's in my life
Unfortunately and unchangeably so

And she doesn't nag
She screams
Yells
Booms
At me

And it's not like she's yelling for me to look both ways
Or to straighten up
It's to do for her
And to live for her
And to help her
For no reason other than she has 'earned' it

She's a leech sucking the will to live from me
She's a road block keeping me from happiness
She's the thick cloud blocking the sun
And worst of all
She's not just in my head anymore

G-Wednesday, December 14th, 2016~Day 183

Any day I don't move is a good one

Any day I eat nothing but ice cream is a good one
Because if I move then I have to think
And if I think
Then I'm just launching myself onto a never-ending hamster wheel
Turning in circles until I dizzy myself

So today
Screw everything else
I make no promises of what to do
I make no plans to change my situation
I'm just going to lay here for as long as it takes to be okay

G-Thursday, December 15th, 2016~Day 184

I've longed to drag my feet across a stage and dance
Even if I'm a bit limited in my element
I know I did my best
I know that as soon I faced the empty audience
The next few months would reward me

And I am ready more than anything
To bring one last bow to my memory
To see the curtain close one last time

Not the last time I'll walk across a stage
But definitely the most memorable

R- Friday, December 16th, 2016 ~Day 185

I have hopes now that the musical is starting up again; I think maybe too much down time has made me think too much overall and that's why everything's been so negative lately. I think more distractions are more of a necessity than before, since I'm kind of combating this on my own and all. I don't know anymore, whether I'm doubtful or hopeful, I've just been mulling through the motions up to this point.

G-Saturday, December 17th, 2016~Day 186

I've done myself up
Like everyday should begin
And I've fluttered longer lashes
At someone who wasn't there

Just for the hell of it
Just because

I don't do a lot of 'just because'
It seems silly to me
It seems like a waste

But trust me this was not wasted
This was a distraction
And a good one
And I think I did a pretty nice job if I do say so myself

G-Sunday, December 18th, 2016~Day 187

I woke up happy?
I don't know
The jury's still out

But I was comfortable when I opened my eyes
I smiled
And I felt like doing something
Anything
Shoot, everything if I could help it

But I still don't know where I'll start

G- Monday, December 19th, 2016~Day 188

Don't know where I'm going
And I don't know how I got here
But I feel a smile on my face
And I'm starting to know my place

And even though I've tried
I feel like I can fly
Because this one day
Ain't starting too bad

And I know it's a long haul
But I'll give it my all
And I'll try and try and try and try again
Because
That's the only way I'll win

G-Tuesday, December 20th, 2016~Day 189

I've treated myself today
I lived like there's no other way
A heavy head won't keep me down
Some rewards lift me off the ground

And nothing stood in my way
I wish other days were like today
I indulged in happiness
I saw others doing their best
I felt that joy
I saw some light
I didn't have to fight tonight

I'll sleep easy
Won't rest hungry
Will do it all again
Because nothing today was like how it's been

R- Wednesday, December 21st, 2016~Day 190

As always I'm cautiously optimistic because even the bad days aren't completely bad. I haven't felt close to the brink in a long time, and I'm not trying my luck with that anytime soon. Maybe. MAYBE it won't all be so bad. But hey, 10 days left and it hasn't gotten worse.

G-Thursday, December 22nd, 2016~Day 191

I'm dealing with my fate
And I know just what I've been dealt
And I hope that it's all worth it
All this excitement that I felt

And I know it won't be easy
But I'll make it either way
And I'm sure that I'll survive it
Since this goes beyond today

And the future is looking so bright
I know when it comes time for that night
I'll be waiting
I'll be watching
And I'll know I did the right thing
And that is all I need
To go home happy
At least for today

G-Friday, December 23rd, 2016~Day 192

I got what I wanted
All covered in red
A new world in a novel
Just what I hoped for

And it was crowded
And I was hungry
For that satisfaction I need
And I know that
I bought for me
But that's all I cared about

I was glad that I came out

If the world I know
Is as warm as this Christmas I'll be glad

G-Saturday, December 24th~Day 193

On this day, every year I'm reminded
That Dysfunctional does not come with an inability to function
Since traditions can stick within our sticky webbed compound
And somehow the tree never falls
No matter how loud and earth shattering the screams get

The only time that really fills me with joy
Just from a memory
Because there is always one good thing about the year before
Or the years before
Since the last wasn't so great

Every year is the tree
Colorful and bright
And warm when my fingers squeeze the bulbs momentarily

I can always remember turning off all of the lights
Watching pebbles of color on the walls
Shaking the plastic pine needles to make them dance
Reading under the tree
Practically living beneath it
Since nothing was so practical every other day

But none of that mattered
As long as we had a tree
And something, anything, to put under it

G- Sunday, December 25th, 2016~ Day 194

My cheeks smiled on their own this morning
My face tingling from face masks
And my magical box of gifts flashed kisses at me as I walked by

My hair was platinum with bananas
And clung together with the smell of shampoo
And in the dark the tree glared on the blank tv screen

And it was quiet
So so so quiet
The quietest it's been without being alone
But it's a good quiet
It doesn't scream anything in its presence

R-Monday, December 26th, 2016~Day 195

I'm not sure how I feel only having five days left. It'll probably be weird not stressing about this every day, not writing so much either. I'm relieved and kind of bummed it'll be over soon, but I think I've had a great first run. I definitely want to do this again, so we'll see. Maybe next time my hope will all be worth it. It was a great Christmas, and a pretty good 195 days so far. Holy crap.

-Tuesday, December 27th, 2016~Day 196

It's so hard seeing such a pretty face cover a cold heart
So very difficult to want to hug warm arms
But recoil at the thought of being embraced by evil itself

I can't deny that there is beauty here
But I also could never doubt that the infatuation I have with it will not last.
I want to be making this up
Want to be exaggerating
But I honestly couldn't if I tried

And everyone else can only see the shiny exterior
Can't get past the glittering perfume defense
And Jewelry clad armor
But I will never forget what rots inside
That which has caused so much of me to shrink

B-Wednesday, December 28th~Day 197

I've shed countless tears
And hated all that fell
But none have ever been so violent
None have left me shaking into a pillow

But none have ever come unprovoked this way
But with knowledge comes despair
And I know too much now

-Thursday, December 29th, 2016~Day 198

I've been talking to air
Though there are people hearing what I'm saying
But not ever listening
I'm talking to air

So I decided that I am through with air
And that I do not deserve this
So I promise to leave all the air behind
Then suddenly I am listened to

So I cover my tracks
Pretend as though air is none of my concern
Just to have it suffocate me later on

Life is funny that way

G-Friday, December 30th, 2016~Day 199

Contrary to popular belief
I love being alone
It's the lonely part that kills you

But not today
Today is a concert through empty hallways
And feasts from the comfort of bed sheets
And excitement for what's to come tomorrow
The last day of this god-awful year
So why not celebrate??

Secret adventures
Giddy excitement trickling through my veins & limbs
How could I feel any better?????

R-Saturday, December 31st, 2016~ Day 200 ♥

Today was the final day. It's a pretty lucky coincidence that it falls on the last day of the year, so I'm glad for that. Today was magical with a dash of terror, but I'd do it ten more times; there was no better way to spend the last night of the year than with such wonderful people. These have been 200 of the worst, most emotional and enlightening days of my life. Even after all of the good I can't deny that this is just part of a year, and I have spent years living this way in such back and forth, but after getting down every moment, every day, all I can do is hope that everything I have told helps someone to help themselves or someone else. At the end of 200 days I gave up on trusting people in charge, gave up on a nation I was raised in, gave up on figuring out what it means to love someone in any way. Instead I decided. I decided to pour myself in the memories I have left to make, the future I want to build, and the support system I have to cherish for the rest of my life. I don't know where I'll go from here, or if I'll even go somewhere that isn't down, but I'm glad to end this journey and move on to the next.